Right Start Right Finish

Buddhism

Anandapanyo Bhikkhu

Copyright © 2015 by Neecha Thian-Ngern.

All rights reserved.

No part of this book may be used or reproduced in any manner whatsoever without written permission except in the case of brief quotations embodied in critical articles or reviews.

For information, address 309 Northwood Drive,
South San Francisco, CA 94080,
or email: neecha.thianngern@gmail.com

Cover Design
Tanawat Pisanuwongse

ISBN: 978-1-935207-18-4
Retail Price: $10.95

Table of Contents

BUDDHISM

What is Buddhism?	2
Is Buddha a God?	4
Is Buddhism a religion or a philosophy?	7
How do Buddhists view other religions? Do they view other religions as wrong?	10
Enlightened beings?	14
What do I need to do to become a Bodhisattva?	17
What are the different schools of Buddhist thought?	22

MAHAYANA

What is Mahayana Buddhism?	24
How many major orders are there in Mahayana Buddhism?	25

THERAVADA

What is Theravada Buddhism?	27
Where did Theravada teachings come from?	28
Are the Theravada Buddhists in Thailand the same as the Theravada Buddhists in other countries?	29
How many major orders are there in Thai Theravada Buddhism?	31
Why did you decide on Theravada Buddhism over other sects?	33

TEACHINGS

What did the Buddha teach?	46
What is the Middle Path?	48
What are the Four Noble Truths?	51

Does the Noble Eightfold Path have to be followed in succession?   61

I've heard people say Sila, Samadhi, Pañña while others say Pañña, Sila, Samadhi. Which is the right order? Does it matter?   66

How can I know whether my perception is a right view or a wrong view?   68

What does Buddhism teach that is different from all other religions?   73

What and where is Nibbana?   74

What does Anatta mean? How can there be No Self?   77

What is meant by Dukkha (suffering)?   79

How does one achieve enlightenment?   80

Are there still enlightened people in this world? How can you tell?   84

I'M ALMOST READY

How can I become a Buddhist?   88

Do I have to believe in everything the Buddha taught in order to be a Buddhist?   91

How can we live a happy and harmonious life through Buddhism?   94

I am interested in Buddhism because I heard it will make me more compassionate and have loving-kindness. Is this true?   100

I'm not good at reading textbooks and scriptures. Do I need to do a lot of studying to practice Buddhism?   110

I hear a lot of Buddhists talk about Abhidhamma. What is it? Do I need to know about it?   116

I have a problem with believing in rebirth, since there is no physical or scientific evidence of an afterlife.   119

I often hear Buddhists talk about letting things go. How does one just simply let it go? It sounds so simple but is so hard to do.   124

BUDDHISM IN ACTION

Father issues   129

McDonald's   135

Post-it note   143

About the Author

Acknowledgments

Chapter One

BUDDHISM

WHAT IS BUDDHISM?

BUDDHISM IS A RELIGION/PHILOSOPHY that is based on the teachings of Gautama Buddha. It is a spiritual practice that leads to the uncovering of the Truth.

Buddhism teaches that it is because we do not recognize the Truth that we have stress and suffering in our lives. All of our problems come from a clear and precise cause — our desires. Our quest to achieve our desires leads to suffering all along the path. Once we recognize the Truth, we can take steps to destroy the cause of our stress and suffering and arrive at the cessation of suffering.

The main goal of Buddhism is to strive towards the elimination of our own suffering and to minimize the suffering we cause others. Causing suffering for others in turn causes more suffering for us.

IS BUDDHA A GOD?

BUDDHA NEVER PROFESSED TO be a god, a descendent of a god, or a messenger of god. Nor do his teachings imply that he is a god. Buddha was a perfected human being. He spent many lives cultivating virtues and in his last life, all his virtues were at the highest possible level.

There can only be one Buddha at a time. Each Buddha only comes during times in which suffering is prevalent in the world. Buddhas come for the purpose of achieving their own enlightenment first and then sharing that knowledge of liberation with people who are ready to achieve enlightenment themselves.

We respect and venerate the Buddha because without him, we would not be able to find the path to ultimate enlightenment. Many people in every era search for a way to escape suffering and find a meaning to life. The Buddha's appearance in this world and his teaching of the Truth is the greatest gift we can receive leading to those ends.

After the Buddha entered Parinibbana (Nirvana), Buddhism gradually disappears from the world. Buddhism itself gradually deteriorates and the teachings get muddied with personal opinions, politics, greed, and desire of power. Eventually, the true teachings of the Buddha are mixed with opinions of regular people and the religion is infected with non-Truths. People in later generations have to work harder to decipher the Truth from the non-Truths. Fewer people will become enlightened. Eventually, enlightened people will cease to exist. The world will once again fall into darkness, unable to find and comprehend basic Truths that will lead away from suffering. After a considerable amount of time and an extensive state of suffering, the need arises for a Buddha to grace the world again. At that point, another Buddha will be born, uncover the Truth, and profess it to those who are willing and able to hear it.

IS BUDDHISM A RELIGION OR A PHILOSOPHY?

......

MANY PEOPLE TRY TO CLASSIFY Buddhism as either a religion or a philosophy. The definition or classification depends on how the individual interprets it. Some people take Buddhism as their refuge, professing unwavering faith, practicing and maintaining traditions, ceremonies, and customs, and using this as their channel to access Buddhism. They identify themselves as Buddhists and find social and personal identity from this classification. For these people, Buddhism acts more as a religion and a way of life.

Others use Buddhism as a representation of their inner beliefs and spirituality. They embrace the law of karma, the Noble Truths, and the existence of spirituality. Some believe there can be many interpretations of truths and ideas. For these people, Buddhism is more a philosophy to be discussed and debated.

For a small group of others, Buddhism is merely a vessel that carries the truths necessary in order to free themselves from the web of suffering and rebirth. These people take the teachings of the Buddha, the Truths of the Dhamma, and the methods used by the Holy Sangha (enlightened followers of the Buddha) and strive to achieve a personal, empirical, and unadulterated understanding of the Truth as it exists in this world as a means to free themselves from their suffering. For these people, whether Buddhism is a religion or philosophy is not important. Rather, they see Buddhism as a collection of teachings that expresses the way out of the cycle of rebirth and suffering.

The truth is that Buddhism is simply a way of thinking, a way of life. Buddhism has aspects of both religion and philosophy. However, Buddhism is neither solely a philosophy nor solely a religion.

Because Buddhists do not worship a creator god or worship the Buddha as a god, many people do not consider Buddhism a religion.

Since Buddhism relies on Truths that can be experienced by all living beings and not on theories and speculations, Buddhism cannot fully be considered a philosophy.

Buddhism is what you want it to be, what you make of it.

HOW DO BUDDHISTS VIEW OTHER RELIGIONS? DO THEY VIEW OTHER RELIGIONS AS WRONG?

BUDDHISTS BELIEVE THAT ALL human beings have the ability and potential to liberate themselves from their own suffering. What the Buddha taught was Truth, not just Buddhist Truth, but universal Truth. Universal Truths are true for all beings, regardless of sex, creed, religion, age, species, or any other factor. All living beings are on a path, a path that encounters suffering every step of the way. At the end, there is cessation of suffering. Each human being is only responsible for their journey, their path.

We cannot judge a religion based on the actions of its followers. All followers are merely human beings. All human beings are fallible. That is our nature. Therefore, we will make mistakes. Those mistakes belong solely to the individual who makes them. That individual is responsible for their mistakes and the results that come from them, not the religion. Therefore, we must be careful lest we judge a religion based on its followers. If all followers acted properly and harmoniously, what need would we have for religion?

The Catholic Church had a scandal with sexual molestation of young boys. However, not all priests do this. Islam is under fire for being a terrorist religion, yet the actual terrorists are a small and extreme group of radical Muslims. The majority of Muslims are not violent and do not condone acts of terror. Hitler was German and killed many Jews, yet not many Germans profess a hatred of Jews. African-Americans were once slaves in the United States. Even though there still exist groups of extremists (like the Ku Klux Klan), the majority of Americans do not hate

African-Americans. In the past, homosexuality was considered an abomination and was punishable by death. Now, in the United States, homosexual couples are allowed to marry. Even in Buddhism, there have been scandals. Some monks over-indulged in their money and power and made international headlines. For example, there is a monk in Sri Lanka who promotes and condones the killing of Muslims.

There have been many religions in the history of the world, and there will be many more. A religion is basically people's best attempt at understanding the world and the Truths and suffering inherent to our existence. Who are we to judge each person's effort at alleviating suffering?

Most of the religions that exist in the current era exist for the purpose of trying to teach people to live better lives and to be better people. They provide guidelines and rules for proper action and speech. They teach their followers to strive to do good for various different reasons.

Buddhism (as originally taught by the Lord Buddha) is the only religion that teaches a step beyond doing good and bettering oneself. Most religions teach heaven as the final destination. Buddhism teaches that heaven is not the final destination, merely a temporary pleasurable rest stop in the cycle of rebirth.

ENLIGHTENED BEINGS?

IN THERAVADA SCRIPTURES, THE BUDDHA defines four types (levels) of enlightenment:

Sotapanna (Stream-Enterer)
Sakadagami (Once-Returner)
Anagami (Non-Returner)
Arahant (Fully Enlightened, a person who has attained nirvana)

As for Arahants, there are 3 different types of Arahants:

1. Disciple Arahant — one who achieves Nirvana under the guidance of a teaching Buddha and is not capable of reaching enlightenment without a teaching Buddha.

2. Paccekabuddha — one who can achieve Nirvana on his own, without the guidance of a teaching Buddha. However, the Paccekabuddha remains silent and does not let his path or method be known unto others. This is either due to his own choice to not teach, or a lack of suitable students at that time.

3. Samma Sambuddho — a perfectly enlightened one. He attains enlightenment on his own, without the help of any Buddhas. In addition, he teaches and trains all sentient beings who are willing to listen.

The Bodhisattva is a being who voluntarily forgoes his own enlightenment and decides to strive for Samma Sambuddho. He will be born many lives and never reach enlightenment until his very last life in which he will become the Samma Sambuddho and achieve enlightenment on his own and then teach the Dhamma to the beings in that era.

WHAT DO I NEED TO DO TO BECOME A BODHISATTVA?

According to Mahayana scriptures, an individual must practice the "six perfections" of giving, moral discipline, patience, effort, concentration, and wisdom in order to fulfill the goal of becoming a Bodhisattva.

According to Theravada scriptures and teachings from various enlightened monks of our era (Acariya Mun, Acariya Thoon), in order to become a Bodhisattva, one must first create enough paramita (cultivation of virtues) to warrant Arahantship. Then, in the presence of a current Buddha, they must make a massive offering of merit and dedicate that merit to achieving their goal of becoming a Bodhisattva. Then, that current Buddha must use his Divine Eye to look into the future and see if this individual will eventually succeed in his goal to become a future Buddha. If there is enough merit and paramita, the Buddha will give the guarantee that this individual will be a future Buddha. The current Buddha will foretell of the era in which the Bodhisattva will achieve Buddhahood and also tell of various details of the future Buddha's dispensation. From that point on, the Bodhisattva will only be reborn as a male and never as an animal smaller than 5 inches.

The current Buddha Gautama recounted his own foretelling of his Buddhahood.

In a past life, he was born as a young man named Sumedha. In that life, he was a rich Brahman who grew disgusted with the world, and cast off his assets and clothing and determined to live a holy life as a hermit. In that era, the Buddha Dipankara had arisen and was teaching sentient beings to become enlightened. The ascetic Sumedha, through his own strivings and meditation practice, achieved supernatural powers such as flight. One day, while traveling through the air, he saw great preparation being made for some grand event and decided to descend to see what was going on. When he learned that the great Buddha Dipankara was to pass by this road, he thought it was a great opportunity for him. Everyone had prepared great gifts to offer to the Buddha Dipankara, but the Ascetic Sumedha had nothing with himself to give. There was a small stretch of road that was not cleared of the previous days rains in time for the great Buddha's passing. When Sumedha saw this, he made the determination to offer his body to prevent the perfect being from muddying his feet on the dirty ground. The ascetic Sumedha lay down in the mud, stretched his hair out to cover all the mud, and allowed the great Buddha and his disciples to step over his body and hair as to prevent them from dirtying their feet. As the great Buddha and his retinue of disciples stepped over him, Sumedha made his aspiration and resolved to become a Buddha for the purpose of bringing salvation to all beings.

The Buddha Dipankara, with his perfect insight and Divine Eye, saw that Sumedha had the heart of a Bodhisattva in training and was a great being on the way to enlightenment. Had Sumedha desired Arahantship, he would have obtained it on the spot. Instead, Sumedha made the determination to delay his own personal enlightenment until he could come back as a future Buddha and lead other beings to enlightenment as well. The Buddha Dipankara approached Sumedha and prophesized that in the far and distant future, many aeons and lifetimes away, Sumedha would eventually be reborn as Prince Siddhartha, born to King Suddhodana and Queen Maya in the forests of Lumbini. He foretold of Prince Siddhartha's renunciation and quest for self-liberation. He told of where and how he would eventually achieve enlightenment, and of the path that Buddha Gautama would teach that would lead to the realization of enlightenment for many beings both during and after the Buddha Gautama's life. He also told of his closest disciples, born as Kolita and Upatissa, and his closest friend, Ananda. He told of many details that would occur in the far off future, including how long Buddha Gautama's religion would last, down to the detail of how he would enter Final Nibanna. At this point, the ten-thousandfold worlds all made a joyous exclamation at the same time, many signs and miracles occurred, and all the worlds shook, as is the case when a future Buddha is foretold.

After that life, Sumedha was officially a Bodhisattva and spent countless lives perfecting the Ten Paramita, as is a prerequisite for all Buddhas.

WHAT ARE THE DIFFERENT SCHOOLS OF BUDDHIST THOUGHT?

THERE ARE MANY DIFFERENT schools of Buddhist thought. The two largest are:

　Mahayana
　Theravada, also known as "Hinayana"

Chapter Two

MAHAYANA

WHAT IS MAHAYANA BUDDHISM?

LITERALLY MEANING THE **"GREAT VEHICLE,"** Mahayana Buddhism is prominent in Northern Asian countries like Tibet, Korea, Japan, China, and Mongolia. Mahayana denotes the path of the Bodhisattva, or future Buddha, who delays his own enlightenment in order to help other others attain it as well. Mahayana is the largest tradition of Buddhism today.

HOW MANY MAJOR ORDERS ARE THERE IN MAHAYANA BUDDHISM?

THERE ARE EIGHT ORDERS in Mahayana Buddhism: Madhyamaka, Yogacara, Tiantai, Huayan, Zen, Pure Land, Esoteric Buddhism, and Nichiren.

Chapter Three

THERAVADA

WHAT IS THERAVADA BUDDHISM?

....

THERAVADA BUDDHISM IS THE OLDEST form of Buddhism that is believed to have descended directly from the Buddha Gautama. Theravada Buddhists adhere mainly to the direct teachings of the Buddha as transcribed by Arahants who personally witnessed his teachings.

WHERE DID THERAVADA TEACHINGS COME FROM?

Theravada Buddhism draws its teachings directly from the Tipitaka, or Pali Canon. Most scholars agree that the Tipitaka is the earliest record of the Buddha's teachings. The Tipitaka is a collection of canons that came directly from Arahant witnesses of the Buddha's teachings. Theravada Buddhism is the main religion in many countries in Southeast Asia, including Thailand, Cambodia, Sri Lanka, Burma, and Laos.

ARE THE THERAVADA BUDDHISTS IN THAILAND THE SAME AS THE THERAVADA BUDDHISTS IN OTHER COUNTRIES?

No, the Theravada community in Thailand is governed and run by the Thailand Theravada Sangha. The head of the Sangha is the Sangharaja (literally Sangha King), who is also referred to as the Supreme Patriarch of Thai Theravada Buddhism. The committee of Sangha Elders, overseen by the Sangharaja, governs and presides over Theravada Buddhism in Thailand. While this is officially the case, most temples and communities effectively govern themselves. When a major issue arises, then the Committee of Sangha Elders are called upon to take an official stance.

In Burma, there is a separate council of Sangha Elders led by their own respective Sangharaja. The same goes for Cambodia and many other Southeast Asian Theravada Buddhist Countries.

HOW MANY MAJOR ORDERS ARE THERE IN THAI THERAVADA BUDDHISM?

In Thailand, there are two major Theravada orders. The larger order is known as Maha Nikaya and the smaller order is known as Dhammayut or Dhammayuttika Nikaya. The Dhammayut Order was a reform movement within the larger order. It was established by Prince Mongkut, who was a monk for many years until later becoming King Rama IV of Thailand. The Dhammayut Order exists in both Thailand and Cambodia.

Prince Mongkut ordained as a monk and observed significant discrepancies between the rules originally laid out by the Buddha in his Vinaya (Monastic Rules of Discipline) and the current practices of the majority of Thai monks. He then sought to use his influence to upgrade the monastic discipline to make it more orthodox. Over the years, he tried to remove all non-Buddhist, supernatural elements including fortune telling, spiritual possessions, luck changing, and karma manipulation. The monks of his new order were known as Dhammayut monks. They were expected to eat only one meal a day, and that meal was to be gathered on a daily alms round. In the present day, many famous Arahant monks belong to the Dhammayut Order, which is also widely known as the forest monk tradition. Their robes are generally a hue of brown as opposed to the robes of the Maha Nikaya, which are usually a hue of orange.

Thailand's present day Theravada Buddhism is home to many new small orders, such as Dhammakaya and Santi Asoka.

WHY DID YOU DECIDE ON THERAVADA BUDDHISM OVER OTHER SECTS?

THERE ARE A LOT OF SECTS of Buddhism to choose from. Each one has their particular strengths and goals. Choosing a sect is an important decision and should be made very carefully. You should clearly identify your personal goals and then research each of the sects you might be interested in. Then, try out each group and see which is the best fit for you.

I was raised by Thai-Buddhist parents, so I was born into Thai Theravada Buddhism. At a young age, I was taught to pray, bow, and participate in various ceremonies. Most of my time was spent in Thai Maha Nikaya Theravada temples. As I got older, I started to have a lot of questions. Most of the questions dealt with reasons behind the ceremonies and the point of various activities and practices. A lot of the answers I received were unsatisfactory to me. However, to be fair, I mostly asked for the opinions of temple visitors, relatives, and other adults. The answers I got left me with more questions. I mostly participated in the ceremonies and activities out of a sense of duty and obligation to my culture and mostly to my mom.

As I got older, my mom gave me the choice to pick my own religion. I went off and studied Christianity and a few of their sects. I read up on various other religions and eventually decided none of them were what I was looking for. I decided my only other choice was atheism. I remained religion-less for most of high school. I went to church with my Christian friends and I went to temple with my family.

Around the time I went off for college, my mom met a new Buddhist teacher named

Acariya Thoon. He was a forest monk from the Dhammayut Order of Thai Theravada. He taught a very sensible and practical way of practicing Buddhism. One of the things that I didn't like about Buddhism until that point was that I was not good at sitting meditation or emptying my mind of thoughts. I had questions I wanted answered. As my mom progressed in this new teacher's teachings, I began to see huge positive changes in her and many of her fellow practitioners. This peaked my curiosity. I began to pay attention during sermons and discussion groups. I found their teaching and practice style to be something I could see myself enjoying. At this point, I joined the group and studied Buddhism for myself.

Acariya Thoon was the only one to teach the Dhamma in a clear and simple way. He taught that we create our suffering through a collection of thoughts and beliefs. The beliefs and thoughts come from a core misunderstanding of reality and the way it truly exists. Therefore, we must first investigate our beliefs and compare them to universal Truths (impermanence, not-self, suffering). Since we are the creators of our beliefs, we must work backwards to dissect and revisit our views. In addition, we must learn to recognize the suffering that comes from our wrong beliefs. Once we know that our beliefs are wrong, and we identify the belief that should replace them, and we know the suffering that comes from our wrong views, we will simply free ourselves from the darkness with the light that is our new understanding and wisdom.

Acariya Thoon taught that meditation is not the main way to practice Dhamma. Instead, cultivation of wisdom in every position, situation, and moment of life is the heart of Dhamma practice. He spoke to what I felt: too many people were just saying "let it go," or that they didn't feel angry or mad, yet their actions proved otherwise. I never believed they let things go as they said. Acariya Thoon taught that only through investigating our viewpoints can we actually let go of them. No amount of meditation or ceremonies can unlock our viewpoints; this must be done volitionally, methodically, and purposefully.

After hearing his views and methods of practice, I tried following Acariya Thoon's teachings. I compared his teachings to what actually transpired in the Buddha's time regarding various enlightened individuals. There were many examples of people who did not know sila (morality, precepts). There were many people who did not study scriptures (there were no scriptures at that time). There were many people who did not meditate at all. Yet all these people were able to become enlightened. Since my goal was enlightenment, I was determined to follow what enlightened people did in the time of the Buddha. I found the path I was born to take.

As I read the Buddha's history, I was astonished at his journey. I was overwhelmed by his sacrifice for our welfare. He spent innumerable lifetimes cultivating his Paramita (Virtues) in order to be a Buddha just so that he could leave teachings for people who were still lost, like me. As I read his Jataka (Birth) stories, it was apparent how much suffering he endured in order to become enlightened for the sake of all beings. I was amazed by his compassion, loving-kindness, and sacrifice. I knew that he was someone worthy of my respect and my veneration. I also knew that it was a path that I could not take. I decided that the best way for me to worship him and practice Buddhism was to strive to become an enlightened being as he was.

The Buddha showed the way to enlightenment and freedom from suffering. He left his palace as a prince and became an ascetic. Many people saw his actions as selfish. However, I saw that he did not leave out of pure selfishness, but rather so that he could better himself and then return and be more qualified to help others. I was inspired by this action. I aspired to better myself with the understanding that by bettering myself, I would be eliminating the causes of suffering (my perceptions) and therefore become a better person. In becoming a better person, I would be helping others by not continuing to be as flawed a person.

As I studied more and more, one thing became brazenly apparent. I was fed up and had enough of this world. I no longer wanted to come back even for one more life. The suffering and Truths that I learned and experienced taught me a lasting lesson. I would strive for this life to be my last.

I was aware that some Buddhists strive to become Buddhas in order to help other beings. I deeply appreciate their dedication and sacrifice. But I could not bear to keep coming back to this world and experienceing all the suffering. I have had enough.

I began practice as a layperson and gradually my life got better. I identified and dealt with my bad behavior, and each day was a valuable lesson. Then, my greatest lesson came when Acariya Thoon passed away. This showed me that life is short and impermanent. It also showed me to not waste any more time. Four months after his cremation ceremony, I ordained as a Thai Theravada Buddhist monk in the Dhammayut (forest monk) Order.

I am on my path for final enlightenment: not for my parents, not for my friends or for anyone else.

I have come to see this world as a never-ending cycle of suffering, of inequality, of injustice. Every extra moment I spend in this cycle of rebirths is a risk — a risk of more pain, a risk of more suffering, a risk of more loss, a risk of creating more karma. I strive for the cessation of my suffering as soon as possible.

As a layperson, I wanted my girlfriends to be a certain way, act a certain way, think a certain way, and speak a certain way. I wanted my mother to be a certain way. I wanted my father to be a certain way. I wanted my sister to be a certain way. When in school, I wanted my teachers to be a certain way. Overall, I truly did not get what I wanted. No matter how much I begged or pleaded, forced or coerced others, I rarely got my way. And even when I did, it was not "exactly" how I wanted it. Many people have tried to change me. They tried force. That didn't work. They tried pressure. That didn't work either. They tried love and kindness. That also didn't work. In the end, I learned one valuable lesson: A person will only change once they truly want to. No other person or people can force or affect true lasting change in another being.

In the end, I learned that if I desired to change others, or change this world according to my desires, I would be met with suffering. I was inspired by the Buddha and many of his foremost disciples. Especially so by his two more foremost students, Venerable Sariputta and Venerable Mahamoggalana. As laymen, they were named Upatissa and Kolita. They were both born into wealthy, prominent families. In their youth, they feasted, partied, and spent their lives in the pursuit of pleasure. Upon visiting a festival for seven days, they progressively observed how the pleasures they received from watching the show diminished. They observed the suffering behind the scenes. They saw how they were no different in the way they were spending their lives, chasing temporary pleasures. They both grew disenchanted with this lifestyle and decided to renounce their lavish lives and find a holy path to the elimination of suffering. Eventually, they made their way to the Buddha and became Arahants.

The same goes for Venerable Mahakassapa who as a layperson had the name Pippali. He grew up in the Brahman caste and was surrounded by wealth and luxury. He was to be married to a beautiful girl named Bhadda. However, both Pippali and Bhadda had no wish to be married and both wanted to live a religious life upon completion of their duties toward their parents. However, they both agreed to marry, per their respective parents' wishes. After they married, they both expressed the aspiration to live a religious life, and both happily agreed to maintain lives of celibacy. One day, as Pippali was overseeing his farms, he saw that as the hands picked the fruit, birds were flying in and eating the worms in the dirt. Pippali asked who would have to pay for this karmic retribution. The clear answer was, him. Because of his wealth, because of his ownership, he would have to take karmic responsibility for the death and suffering of many lives. Shaken by this realization, he aspired to give away all his wealth and ordain. When he tried to give the wealth to his wife, she also refused and wanted to ordain. They both agreed to give away their fortune and go their separate ways in search of a holy life.

Upatissa and Kolita, as well as Pippali and Bhadda, realized the suffering and futility of life in this world. Their only remaining desire was to search for a way to free themselves from this karmic cycle, from the seemingly unending cycle of suffering and pain. Once they found 'The Way', through the Buddha's instructions, they dedicated themselves to non-stop practice, doing whatever it took to achieve their goals. Once they were Arahants, they spent the rest of their lives helping the Buddha teach and spread the Dhamma to all who would listen.

I want to help people and affect good change in the world around me. If I do not first learn to properly help myself and find my own enlightenment, what would I have to teach and help others? If I remain flawed and ignorant, then my help and teachings will be marred by my ignorance and flaws. I would be hurting others more than I would be helping them.

This is akin to someone who has yet to learn how to swim and jumps into the water to save a drowning person. In the end, both people are unlikely to survive. The drowning person will die, but now, the helper will also die, because he does not have the ability to save himself, let alone the drowning person. So instead of one person drowning, now there are two.

This is also akin to a person trying to give CPR. As most doctors, nurses, firefighters, paramedics, and other trained individuals know, a person who is not trained to give CPR could actually do more harm than good. They could actually collapse the lung or break the ribs of the person they are intently trying to help. In fact, they could end up killing the individual they set out to help.

The lesson I take from this is that before helping others, one must first learn to help oneself. That is mainly why I choose to walk this path.

Chapter Four

TEACHINGS

WHAT DID THE BUDDHA TEACH?

PLAIN AND SIMPLE, THE BUDDHA taught the Truth. The Buddha taught that because we cannot see or recognize the Truth, we live our lives with suffering and stress. If we can both know and experience the Truth of the world, we can be free from the cycle of rebirth and the suffering inherent to life.

In his first sermon, the *Dhammacakkavatthana Suttam*, the Buddha taught three main topics to his first five disciples.

He taught:

> Majjhima Patipada – Middle Path
> Four Noble Truths
> Noble Eightfold Path

WHAT IS THE MIDDLE PATH?

IN SIMPLE TERMS, THE MIDDLE PATH basically means moderation. The Buddha taught his disciples to avoid self-indulgence in sensual pleasures and to avoid self-mortification.

Before becoming the Buddha, Prince Siddhartha experienced both extremes. As a prince, Siddhartha had all that could be given or owned; he had a palace for each season, unlimited servants, lavish foods, and access to a wide variety of sensual pleasures. Deep down inside, he knew the way to enlightenment could not be found through sensual pleasures. Siddhartha left the palace and searched for a holy life. At one point, Siddhartha endured torture of the body in the search for enlightenment. He allowed himself to become emaciated to the point where his bones could be seen through his skin. He meditated all day and all night. Siddhartha realized that if he were to continue down this road, the ultimate end would be death. With death, he would merely be reborn without being any closer to enlightenment.

At this point, wisdom and discernment arose in Siddhartha's mind and he understood deeply within his soul that enlightenment can only be gained through the Middle Path, not through sensual pleasures or self-mortification.

For us, we can easily see when we have strayed from the Middle Path. When we eat, we know when we are full. If we were to continue eating, we would not be following the Middle Path. If we were not to eat enough, we would inherently know that we were still hungry, and thus, were not on the Middle Path.

In practice, the Middle Path is very helpful. It can be applied to virtually every situation. If a situation runs afoul, a mistake in the Middle Path can usually be found.

For example, parents want to give their kids things that will make them happy. However, they are afraid of spoiling them. There is a moderation or Middle Path to be followed here.

WHAT ARE THE FOUR NOBLE TRUTHS?

AT THE FIRST SERMON given by the Buddha, the *Dhammacakkavatthana Suttam*, he explained that he came to understand that all things were subject to truths that he labeled as The Four Noble Truths.

The Buddha discovered the Four Noble Truths which are:

1. Life entails suffering

For all beings two types of suffering are clear. There is the physical suffering that we must all endure. The suffering that comes with birth, the suffering that comes from growing old, the suffering that comes with sickness, and the suffering that comes with death. All other physical suffering such as pain and discomfort are included.

In addition to physical suffering that fills our daily existence, there is also the emotional suffering that we experience. The spectrum of emotional suffering is rather wide. Feelings such as fear, distress, stress, anger, irritation (mental), frustration, paranoia, loss, anxiety, depression, annoyance, jealousy, and much more constitute the emotional suffering that comes with our lives.

The Buddha further explained that happiness and enjoyments are the byproducts of the temporary subsiding of suffering. Happiness and bliss cannot exist without suffering as a cause. For example, relief cannot come without previously feeling fear or stress. So simply speaking, life equals suffering.

2. Suffering has a cause which is known to the Buddha

The Buddha, using his comprehensive knowledge and wisdom, discerned that all suffering, both mental and physical, does not spontaneously arise. That is, suffering does not come out of nowhere with no cause. He identified that all the suffering we experience stemmed from a direct cause. That cause is our desires.

Our desires lead us to suffering. The desire to be born leads to the suffering of birth. Birth, in turn, leads to the suffering of growing old, the suffering of sickness and physical deterioration, and the suffering of death.

The desire to have something that someone else has is the cause for jealousy. The desire to have things the way we want is the cause for anger, stress, irritation, and frustration. The desire for things to stay in their current form and not change is the cause for anxiety, anger, loss, and many other feelings.

All of our suffering can be traced to causes that consist of desires.

3. Suffering will end when its cause ends

The Buddha realized that the desires that lead to suffering are voluntary desires. That is, not everyone has the same desires. We each pick and choose (both knowingly and unknowingly) the desires to which we attach ourselves. And then in turn, we experience the suffering inherent to those choices.

Because our suffering comes from choices, there is hope. If we can learn to un-make and un-choose those choices, we can free ourselves from the subsequent suffering.

This Third Noble Truth provides us with hope and is the starting point for Buddhist practice. The goal of Buddhist practice is the elimination of suffering, which we now know comes from the choices that we make. Therefore, if we knew how to make better, more informed choices, we would be subject to less and less suffering.

4. The Buddha has told the path to the end of suffering

The Buddha realized the path to the elimination of suffering. This is the most important Noble Truth. This is the Noble Truth of the Way, the Method, the Medicine. With this Noble Truth, the Buddha gave us the tools to free ourselves from the suffering we experience. He called this method the Noble Eightfold Path.

If we follow the Path correctly and diligently, we will end up with the elimination of our suffering.

The Noble Eightfold Path:

> Right Perception, Right View
> Right Thought
> Right Speech
> Right Action
> Right Livelihood
> Right Effort
> Right Focus
> Right Concentration

The Noble Eightfold Path starts off with Right Perception. All of our thoughts, actions, and speech stem from our perceptions. If our perceptions are wrong, then our thoughts, speech, and actions have absolutely no chance of being right. If our perceptions are right, then we will think, speak, and act correctly. Therefore, having the right perception or right view is critical to thinking, speaking, acting, and living correctly.

If we have the right perceptions, then we can generate right thoughts. These right thoughts will help us have right speech and right action. With right speech and right action, we will be able to generate and maintain a right livelihood. If we think, speak, act, and live right, we will put in right effort. While exerting right effort, we will be rightly focused. Once we are rightly focused, we will be able to have right concentration.

Many people hold the perception that being rich can solve their problems. This is a wrong perception. This perception will lead that person to think of ways to get rich. When they speak, their words will represent their greed, their desire, and their viewpoints that wealth can solve problems. They will say things such as, "We can spend time together once we are rich," or "Once we are rich, everything will get better," or "I only want to hang out with rich people, sorry." These are wrong speech. This type of speech harms yourself and others. Based on your wrong perceptions and wrong thoughts, you will commit wrong actions. You will be willing to do things to get ahead at the cost of hurting others, you will be willing to put money ahead of your family's feelings, or you will be willing to steal or cheat. These are wrong actions since they can hurt both you and others. If you have this as a perception, then you will be willing to have a wrong livelihood. You will live your life for money and be willing to take jobs that are ethically and morally wrong, such as the livelihoods of prostitution, drug dealing, crime, and the sale of humans or animals. These livelihoods hurt both you and others. If you have these perceptions, you will put forth effort, focus, and concentration in accomplishing your goal. However, this goal will not solve your problems and will in fact cause you more suffering. Therefore, this is wrong effort, focus, and concentration. As you can clearly see, this all started with the wrong perception.

There are many other wrong perceptions held by all living beings. It is our job, the purpose of our lives, to seek out these wrong perceptions and recalibrate them with the Truth in order to hold right perceptions.

All living beings are born due to their wrong perceptions. We suffer due to our wrong perceptions. We hurt others and create bad karma based on our wrong perceptions. We try to fix our problems with techniques based on wrong perceptions, and that is why we have been unable to completely fix our problems.

In order to solve our problems, stop hurting others, and live harmoniously with others and within ourselves, we must fix our wrong perceptions. Once we have realigned our wrong perceptions with the Truth, we will experience true freedom, true tranquility, and true happiness.

A Dhamma practitioner offered this personal story:

I have a friend who had a very stressful time at her university. So, after many health and addiction problems, she ended up dropping out of school. She cleaned herself up, got a great job, and was generally happy with her life.

However, she ended up going back to school and encountering the same stress and problems. Once again, she decided to drop out and everything was fine. This happened 5 times over 10 years and each time she experienced significant levels of suffering.

Finally, she realized one day that the thing that was driving her to keep going back to school was the belief that finishing school was critical to being a good, smart, successful person. She believed that to be a productive member of society, she had to have a college degree.

But when she took a good look at her life, at her life's experiences, she realized that this wasn't always true. When she wasn't struggling with school and stress from dropping out, she was a good person, friend, and productive member of society. She was clever and had a job that she loved. Once she saw that her own experiences disproved her view, she let go of the attachment to the idea that without a degree she could not be the ideal person she wanted to be. With her change of view on degrees, her entire cycle of suffering just stopped. There was no longer anything driving her to keep going back to school.

DOES THE NOBLE EIGHTFOLD PATH HAVE TO BE FOLLOWED IN SUCCESSION?

MOST DEFINITELY. THIS IS a very important question. There is a very important reason the Buddha listed out the Noble Eightfold Path in this order. The order listed is the exact way he practiced, himself. Every single enlightened person practiced in this exact order. Every person who is not enlightened has failed to follow the Noble Eightfold Path properly.

The order is given as:

1. Right View/ Right Perception
2. Right Thought

3. Right Speech
4. Right Actions
5. Right Livelihood
6. Right Effort
7. Right Mindfulness
8. Right Concentration

The Noble Eightfold Path can be further split into three groups:

GROUP of WISDOM (Pañña)
1. Right View/Perception
2. Right Thought

GROUP of ACTION (Sila)
3. Right Speech
4. Right Actions
5. Right Livelihood

GROUP of CONCENTRATION (Samadhi)
6. Right Effort
7. Right Mindfulness
8. Right Concentration

Right View MUST come first in every case — no matter what. Without Right View, no practice is correct or fruitful. It is like attempting to travel to a certain location without knowledge of where it is or what it looks like. You will most likely never reach that location no matter how hard you try. Even if you manage to accidentally arrive there, you will have no idea that you are there, and no idea that your journey is over. Therefore, you will continue to journey past your final destination.

From Right View, Right Thought will follow. That is, if you know where you are going, and where it is, you will start to formulate proper plans for arriving at that place. But the plans must be made knowing exactly where the destination is.

From Right View and Right Thought, you must put forth the real physical and verbal actions needed to get to that location. That is, the Right Speech, the Right Actions, and the Right Livelihood. There is no particular order for these three. The only thing is they must come after Right View and Right Thought.

If you have Wrong View, your thoughts will be Wrong Thought. Then the actions (physical and verbal) will come out Wrong Speech, Wrong Action, Wrong Livelihood. If you have wrong directions, when you travel and ask questions, it will all be based on the wrong directions.

From Right View, followed by Right Thought, followed by Right Speech, Right Action, and Right Livelihood, you will put forth Right Effort. That is, you will exert effort in the manner that will lead you closer to your goal. If you followed the Wrong View, Wrong Thought, Wrong Speech, Wrong Action, Wrong Livelihood path, you will also still put forth effort, but it will be Wrong Effort; that is, it is effort that does not lead you to your goal. Instead, it leads you away from your goal. If you have the right directions, and physically start your travel, then you will exert effort, mindfulness, and concentration in the task ahead of you — getting to your goal. If your directions were correct, then your actions will be towards arriving at the proper goal, then all effort, mindfulness and concentration you put forth will be towards arriving at the correct goal. However, if your directions were wrong from the start, the actions you take, the effort and concentration you put forth, will all be for naught, since there is no way you can arrive at your goal.

From Right Effort, you will have Right Mindfulness and Right Concentration. That is, you will be mindful of your journey and concentrate on the journey itself. There is no particular order in Effort, Mindfulness, and Concentration. The only order is that they come after Right View, Right Thought, and Right (GROUP of ACTION).

I'VE HEARD PEOPLE SAY SILA, SAMADHI, PAÑÑA WHILE OTHERS SAY PANNA, SILA, SAMADHI. WHICH IS THE RIGHT ORDER? DOES IT MATTER?

I HAVE ALSO HEARD THIS. Many people nowadays preach Sila first, followed by Samadhi and Pañña. They believe that one must first be virtuous and practice tranquil meditation concentration (samadhi) and then wisdom (pañña) will automatically arise. Acariya Thoon was adamantly against this belief. He dedicated most of his life after becoming an Arahant to dispelling this popular widespread belief. When we asked him where this belief came from, he told us that non-enlightened persons were writing books and teaching people the wrong methods. Since they were not enlightened, they had no way of knowing whether their teachings were right or wrong.

Acariya Thoon taught us that the Buddha himself laid out the Noble Eightfold Path in a very precise and particular order. Yet, only 2550 years later, we have already completely rearranged his teachings. The Buddha taught that we must first identify and practice wisdom properly. Then we will know what is right and what is wrong. We will be unable to do that which is wrong because we will know the consequences of our actions. Our minds will refuse to allow us to do that which will clearly hurt us. Then, through wisdom and morality, we will be at peace and have proper concentration.

So, before we focus on precepts or practice meditation and concentration, we must first identify what is a right view and what is a wrong view. We must first develop wisdom before we can have restraint or concentration.

HOW CAN I KNOW WHETHER MY PERCEPTION IS A RIGHT VIEW OR A WRONG VIEW?

THE **B**UDDHA **PROVIDED US** with a special tool – the Truth. There are three types of Truths:

Individual Truths – Truths that are held by individuals. These are Truths such as – I am always right. I am the victim. I own this or that. Or any statement that begins with "I believe…"

Democratic Truths – Truths that are held by the majority. These truths include:

- Certain drugs or substances are allowed, while others are banned.

- Laws.
- Courts can decide our fates.
- Taxes are fair.

As long as the majority agrees, it is considered a truth. However, not all democratic truths are held by all. In fact, the term majority implies the existence of a minority. If the majority is right, then by definition, the minority must be wrong.

Universal Truth – Truths that are held by all living beings. These Truths include: all beings love their own lives, no being wants to be deprived of what they have, all things change, and all life must eventually die. These Truths are known by all living beings.

If our perception is based on an individual or democratic truth, there is a chance that it might be wrong. For example, individuals have believed themselves to be in the right, even after they have committed a crime. In this case, the individual holds individual truths, but is being punished by democratic truths. In this case, who is right and who is wrong?

To know this, we must be able to discern what is or isn't a universal Truth. The Buddha gave us tools to use for this:

Dukkha
Annicam
Anatta

Dukkha is the Pali word for suffering or stress. Dukkha is the result of our wrong perception that has manifested itself in thoughts, speech, and actions. In this, Dukkha is like a sensor. Once it goes off, we are alerted that we are holding a wrong perception. Dukkha is like the pain we feel in our bodies. The pain receptors we have are there to alert us that something is wrong and steps should be taken to alleviate the pain.

Annicam is the tool to alleviate the pain. Annicam is defined as impermanence. Annicam can also be interpreted as "change", "nothing stays the same", and "everything comes in pairs." The Buddha taught that everything in this world is subject to Dukkha, Annicam, and Anatta. Therefore, we are suffering since we do not see the Annicam in our perceptions. For example, if we are upset that a loved one's personality has changed, this is because we expected their personality not to change. Our expectation for something to always stay the same is contrary to Annicam. We are refusing to allow something to transpire the way it is meant to. Everyone changes, therefore our expectation that they will not, will only be met with suffering, stress, and disappointment.

Anatta is the result of understanding Annicam. Anatta is the cessation of existence in a supposed form. Once a seed has been planted and it sprouts into a young tree, that identity as "seed" is considered to be Anatta. Once the young tree becomes an old tree, the young tree is considered to be Anatta. All that is in the world can only exist for a finite period of time. Therefore, our "self" cannot be in these temporary things. Many Buddhists try to practice and contemplate Anatta (in the form of nothingness). Acariya Thoon taught Anatta should not be contemplated. It will be understood only through the cultivation and understanding of Annicam. This is the same as someone who has not eaten but is contemplating the concept of fullness. Through that contemplation, they will never arrive at fullness. However, through eating (understanding Annicam) they will arrive at fullness on their own. Just as fullness is the end result of eating, Anatta is the end result of Annicam. In this case, Dukkha would be the hunger that alerts us that we should eat.

Perceptions that lead to Dukkha are not Truth. Perceptions that are contrary to Annicam are not Truth. Perceptions that are contrary to Anatta are not Truth.

WHAT DOES BUDDHISM TEACH THAT IS DIFFERENT FROM ALL OTHER RELIGIONS?

BUDDHISM HAS TWO UNIQUE concepts that no other religions have:

Nibbana
Anatta

WHAT AND WHERE IS NIBBANA?

NIBBANA IS THE END OF SUFFERING and happiness. When a person extinguishes the five aggregates, they are said to have attained Nibbana. Nibbana does not exist as a location, and of those who attain Nibbana characteristically do not come back and become reincarnated. No one truly knows precisely what Nibbana is. This is akin to asking where a light goes after the electricity has gone out. No one can explain where it goes, yet it is obvious that there is no more light. All we can know is what we can infer and from what the Buddha told us of Nibbana.

Happiness and suffering alternate. Suffering and happiness are two sides of the same coin. Suffering cannot be avoided without avoiding happiness. Happiness cannot be obtained without obtaining suffering. Therefore, if we no longer have suffering and happiness and neither suffering nor happiness. That is what Nibbana is.

The Buddha said about Nibbana,

"This is peace, this is exquisite — the resolution of all fabrications, the relinquishment of all acquisitions, the ending of craving; dispassion; cessation; Nibbana."
— AN 3.32

"There is that dimension where there is neither earth, nor water, nor fire, nor wind; neither dimension of the infinitude of space, nor dimension of the infinitude of consciousness, nor dimension of nothingness, nor dimension of neither perception nor non-perception; neither this world, nor the next world, nor sun, nor moon. And there, I say, there is neither coming, nor going, nor stasis; neither

passing away nor arising: without stance, without foundation, without support [mental object]. This, just this, is the end of stress."
— *Ud 8.1*

WHAT DOES ANATTA MEAN? HOW CAN THERE BE NO SELF?

ANATTA IS COMMONLY TRANSLATED as "not-self." What this means is cessation of a "self" or identity, cessation of existence in a conventional form, or that ownership cannot exist because all things including owner and object will cease to be.

"Not-self" exists just as "self" does — only for a brief period. Not-self and self are two sides of the same coin. Anything that comes into existence is subject to the three common characteristics, namely, suffering, impermanence, and cessation of being.

Throughout our existence, we are constantly redefining who we are. At one point we call ourselves young. At another, we refute that and say we are not young, but not old. At another stage, we say we are old. At one time, we see ourselves as fat. At other times, we see ourselves as normal. At other times, we see ourselves as too skinny. Sometimes we see ourselves as shy and timid, and at other times, we see ourselves as brave and brash.

We have various identities. We shift and change them all the time. So what are we really? There is no identity that we can define as us. There is no identity that can encompass all that is us. There is no identity that can account for the change, growth, and deterioration we are subject to. Even our names lose value as we are reborn.

This is what the Buddha meant when he said there is no self.

WHAT IS MEANT BY DUKKHA (SUFFERING)?

SUFFERING IS SIMPLY ANY FEELING or state that you would rather not experience. This includes depression, stress, anger, lust, envy, jealousy, annoyance, coughing, weariness, hunger, loneliness, sickness, old age, death, and boredom ....the list can go on practically forever.

Suffering is the whole spectrum of undesirable states.

HOW DOES ONE ACHIEVE ENLIGHTENMENT?

ENLIGHTENMENT MEANS FREEING YOUR MIND from your misperceptions. These misperceptions are the cause of our suffering and the reason we have to keep being reborn. Thus, by developing the right views and practicing proper discernment we will automatically destroy the delusions and wrong views that we hold. Through destroying these wrong views, we free ourselves from having to be reborn.

There are four levels of enlightenment:

> Sotapanna — Stream-Enterer
> Sakadagami — Once-Returner
> Anagami — Non-Returner
> Arahant — Ultimate Enlightenment

Once you become a Stream-Enterer, the results are that you are free from "personality belief" or sense of ego. You no longer have any skeptical doubt about the Buddha, Dhamma, Sangha, Karma, and heaven and hell. You also no longer cling to rituals. You have a deep understanding of right and wrong and therefore, automatically do not break the precepts. Stream-Enterers are no longer subject to rebirths in hell or any of the lower realms. They will only be born in the human realm (as a human) or the fine-sense spheres. They are guaranteed to be on the path to enlightenment. They will experience rebirth no more than 7 times. In their last life, they will obtain full enlightenment and Nibbana.

Once one becomes a Once-Returner, they have accomplished all that a Stream-Enterer has accomplished in addition to nearly being free from sensuous craving and ill-will (hatred, lust for revenge). The Sakadagami will be born at most 3 times, and at the minimum one time. During their last life, they will be guaranteed Nibbana.

Once one becomes a Non-Returner, they have accomplished all that a Once-Returner had accomplished in addition to fully freeing themselves from sensuous craving and ill-will (hatred, lust for revenge). The Anagami will not be reborn in the human world again, but instead be reborn in a higher world and wait for Nibbana.

Once one becomes an Arahant, they have extinguished all the things the Anagami has in addition to craving for fine material existence, craving for immaterial existence, conceit, restlessness and ignorance. An Arahant is a being who has destroyed greed, hatred and delusion. Once fully awakened, the Arahant has attained Nibbana. For the Arahant, there will be no more rebirths anywhere.

Acariya Thoon also taught that for one to become enlightened, one must have sufficient amounts of three things:

1. Past culmination of virtues (Pāramitā)
2. Right Understanding, Right Views (Samma-ditthi)
3. Exertion of Right Effort (Samma-Vāyāmā)

If we find that we are lacking in any particular area, then that is the area we should work on.

ARE THERE STILL ENLIGHTENED PEOPLE IN THIS WORLD? HOW CAN YOU TELL?

THERE IS ONLY ONE WAY to know beyond a shadow of a doubt if someone is enlightened. We can only tell once they have passed away. Once they have passed away and have been cremated, their bones will become relics. However, this only applies to Arahants. Remains of the Anagami, Sakadagami, and Sotapanna will not become relics.

We cannot personally know whether others are enlightened until we have become enlightened ourselves. Once we have obtained enlightenment, we will recognize, through firsthand knowledge, others who are enlightened.

Our teacher, the Venerable Acariya Thoon Khippapanyo, passed away on Nov 11, 2008. Upon cremation, his remains became relics. This certifies that he was an Arahant. Acariya Thoon taught that ariyapuggala (noble persons) still exist in this world. Therefore, it is reasonable to assume that as long as the Buddha's followers are practicing in his footsteps, there can still be enlightened people in this world.

However, it is pointless to try and guess who is enlightened and who is not. Acariya Thoon taught that there are four types of Dhamma Practitioners (adapted from Thai):

1. Dressed as a poor person, actually poor
2. Dressed royally, actually poor
3. Dressed as a poor person, actually wealthy
4. Dressed royally, actually wealthy

In this example, how we are dressed does not necessarily correspond to how we act. Our actual wealth corresponds to our Dhamma knowledge.

We cannot know how much Dhamma knowledge someone has by looking at their behavior. Therefore, it is dangerous to assume whether or not someone has true Dhamma understanding. If you assume incorrectly, you run the risk of exponentially magnifying the faults of your actions.

Chapter Five

I'M ALMOST READY!

Just a few more questions...

HOW CAN I BECOME A BUDDHIST?

THERE ARE MANY WAYS to become a Buddhist. The simplest way is to think like a Buddhist. Use Buddhist thought to solve your problems. Use Buddhist concepts in your life. Such as:

- Tracing the result back to its cause. Everything has a cause. Our problems come from our actions and our speech. Our actions and our speech come from our thoughts. Our thoughts come from our points of view. Therefore, if we learn how to find the true cause of our problems, we have already applied a key concept of Buddhism.

- Focus your attention on yourself. You are the most important person in your world. You make the most mistakes in your world. You are the angriest person in your world. Everyone in the world has so many faults – including you. However, you are the only one whose problems YOU can fix! If you realize this, start devoting time to analyzing YOURSELF and leave others alone. This is a key concept in Buddhism.

- Learn to see cause and effect. All of your speech and actions have a cause. In turn, they themselves are a cause. Learn to be perceptive and notice what effect your speech and actions have. If it is a good effect, continue doing it. If it is a bad effect, take note of this and begin to fix it. Refraining from doing evil and instead practicing doing good is a key concept to Buddhism.

Another way to become a Buddhist is to make an inner commitment to accept the Buddha, Dhamma, and Sangha as your source of spiritual guidance. You do not need to have a formal ceremony in order to be considered a Buddhist. Being a Buddhist is merely a state of mind.

Another way is to merely believe in the religion of Truth. Searching for Truths, living by Truths, and cultivating the understanding of Truths. If you live your life in this manner, you are already living a Buddhist life.

DO I HAVE TO BELIEVE IN EVERYTHING THE BUDDHA TAUGHT IN ORDER TO BE A BUDDHIST?

....

BUDDHISM IS A PRACTICE based on understanding first, believing second. Therefore, as you develop understanding, belief will follow.

The Buddha had the foresight to leave us with the Kalama Sutta:

Kalama Sutta "Do not believe in anything simply because you have heard it. Do not believe in anything simply because it has been handed down for many generations. Do not believe in anything simply because it is spoken and rumored by many. Do not believe in anything simply because it is written in Holy Scriptures. Do not believe in anything merely on the authority of Teachers, elders, or wise men. Believe only after careful observation and analysis, when you find that it agrees with reason and is conducive to the good and benefit of one and all. Then accept it and live up to it." — The Buddha

In many schools, children are taught the telephone game. Everyone sits in a circle. The teacher whispers a phrase to the first child who whispers it to the second child. By the time it gets to the end, the message can be completely transformed.

Similarly so, the Buddha knew that in the future (i.e. our present) people would be presented with many versions and variations of his teachings. He taught that we should be cautious in believing everything we are taught. However, we should not be so skeptical that we believe nothing. We must actively investigate each teaching to see whether it makes sense and is beneficial to us.

Therefore, we do not need to summarily believe in all "Buddhist" teachings. We should begin by studying concepts that we are attracted to and examine the validity of them. Once we have firsthand understanding and experience, we can determine, with our discernment, what is true and what is not.

But just as we should not summarily believe everything religion has taught us, we should also not summarily believe everything our nurture and upbringing has taught us (remember these mistakes: slavery, human sacrifice, and the belief that the world is flat).

HOW CAN WE LIVE A HAPPY AND HARMONIOUS LIFE THROUGH BUDDHISM?

Understanding cause and effect
Buddhism teaches us to find the cause of our problems. Once we find that cause, we can take steps to destroy it. Once the cause is destroyed, our problem will never return. If we have one less problem that will not return, is that not happiness?

Learning about yourself
The more we know about ourselves, the more we will be able to commit to actions, speech,

and thoughts that will truly benefit our lives and bless us with true happiness. True happiness comes from the inside out. We must learn about ourselves. Through learning about ourselves, we begin to understand others.

Compassion and Forgiveness

Compassion and forgiveness are key concepts in Buddhism. However, to give compassion or forgiveness without right view is to merely create a higher sense of ego. To forgive, we must first recollect an instance when we have committed the same type of action. We must first understand the motives justifying our actions and the effects of our actions. Without understanding why we have committed an action, we will not be able to allow others to do the same. Through understanding our own actions, we will be compassionate and forgiving towards others as a result.

For example, if someone cuts in front of you in line, this might make you angry. You might try and calm yourself down by telling yourself that this person:

> Didn't see you
> Is in a hurry
> Is having a bad day

If you try to have compassion or give forgiveness, it will only be given based on a condition. If compassion or forgiveness is based on a condition, it will only stand as long as the condition stands. Therefore, if you find out later that they:

> Did see you
> Were not in a hurry
> Were not having a bad day

You would no longer be able to forgive or have compassion for this person. This is because your forgiveness and compassion was born out of a condition.

In order to truly feel compassion or give forgiveness, you must first understand the action.

Begin by internalizing. Ask yourself: Have I ever done this? (cut in line, taken someone's place) If not, ask yourself a second question: Have I ever done something like this (made others wait, been inconsiderate of others)? Once you find a situation in which you have done it, you will understand firsthand why you did it. You will have empirical knowledge as to the cause and effect of your actions. You will be able to see both sides of the situation. Through this understanding you will understand that there are reasons for this type of action. Then you will be able to generate true forgiveness and true compassion. In addition you will be able to make better decisions and be more aware of the effects of your actions.

True freedom — Living life without conditions
So much of our lives are based on conditions. Conditions, just as everything in the world, are subject to Annicam (change, impermanence). Therefore, if our lives are based on conditions that change, when that change comes, we will experience suffering. We often hear others and (most importantly) ourselves say:

"I would be happier if I had … (a BMW, a new bike, a new girlfriend, more money)"

> We assume that we would be happier if we had a new BMW. But we forget about what comes with it: security issues, gas prices, expensive maintenance, driving people around, people wanting to borrow your car.

"I wouldn't be so mad if she did …. instead of …"

> We think we would not be so mad if others changed their actions or speech. However, even when they say things differently or act differently, we still get mad. This is because the anger stems from perceptions inside of us, not from the actions of others.

"I am so lonely, if only I had someone …"

> We think that our loneliness will be gone if only we had someone. However, even when we have someone, we still feel lonely, regardless of whether they are close by

or not. This is because loneliness comes from the inside.

All these statements are based on conditions. Once the conditions change, our satisfaction and happiness also change. Therefore, learning to live without setting impermanent conditions is the way to a happy life.

I AM INTERESTED IN BUDDHISM BECAUSE I HEARD IT WILL MAKE ME MORE COMPASSIONATE AND HAVE LOVING-KINDNESS. IS THIS TRUE?

Compassion and Loving-Kindness (Metta) are very popular concept in Buddhism. Many people are drawn to Buddhism because of the idea of compassion and loving-kindness.

In fact, many meditation centers have created a form of meditation called metta bhavana (which means the meditation of compassion and goodwill). This practice begins with the meditator generating compassion for oneself, then for one's loved ones, strangers, enemies, and then all beings.

In some other meditation groups, they practice loving-kindness in conjunction with their breathing. Inward breath denotes compassion for oneself and outwards breath denotes compassion for others.

For some others, compassion is generated through the chanting of mantras and Sutras. There are many Sutras that detail wishes for all beings to be free from suffering and stress, and to live contently.

This method is effective in keeping compassion and loving-kindness in the forefront of your mind. It gives you an activity to do that reminds you to be compassionate.

However, meditating and chanting is not the only method effective in affecting long-lasting compassion inside your heart and soul. For many people, just telling yourself to be compassionate is not enough. The hate and anger they feel for others cannot merely be quelled by chants and mantras. Nor can it be replaced by breathing techniques. It is easy to have compassion for people you love or people who create benefit for you. But it is difficult to generate compassion for those that seem to hurt you, or to wish you harm, or that have little positive benefit for you.

The best way to practice true compassion and loving-kindness and have it actually become a lasting part of your soul's psyche is to practice the concept of Opanayiko — which means leading inwards.

OPANAYIKO — leading inwards

In this practice, we teach ourselves to internalize what we see externally and to find examples in our lives that mirror what we see. When we see others fighting and doing ugly things, we should use them as a mirror for ourselves instead of ignoring them, making an excuse for them, or criticizing them. It is easy to see the faults and silliness of the actions of others, however, it is difficult and neigh impossible for most people to see, accept, admit, or acknowledge the faults and silliness of our actions.

For example, in one case, a practitioner in Thailand was upset. She had woken up early and parked her car in front of a bank in a normally crowded shopping center. After finishing her business, she saw that her car was boxed in. She was not mad, because this is the norm in Thailand. It's customary for people to block in another car, as long as they leave the gear in neutral and the parking brake off. That way, if the blocked in car needed to leave, they could just gently push the other car aside. When the practitioner saw the car, she was not immediately mad. She just thought that she would move the car and go home. However, when she went to move the car, she saw that the car would not budge. When she peered inside, she saw that the parking brake was engaged. This made her furious. This meant that she would have to wait until this person got back to move on with her life. No amount of breathing, no amount of chanting or mantras could calm her down. She was ready to explode.

She called one of the nuns at our temple and voiced her frustrations strongly. The nun asked her to practice Opanayiko and try to lead this story inwards, as a parallel to see if she had ever done something like this before. She immediately said, "I have never been so inconsiderate as to block someone's car and leave the parking brake engaged." She was sure she had never done this (many might forget that they HAVE done it), since she had only recently begun to drive and her collection of parking experiences was limited and she was certain that she had never done this to anyone before.

The nun then asked her to expand her field of criteria. Instead of trying to find if she had "blocked someone in with the parking brake engaged," the nun asked the practitioner to expand her scope. What else was the "inconsiderate" person doing to us? The practitioner exclaimed, "he is making me wait for him and wasting my time!" The nun then asked, have you ever done "this" to anyone one before.

When the practitioner thought about it, she realized that she makes other people wait for her quite often. Just that morning she told her husband, brother, sister, and son to wait in the car and she would be out in a minute. She ended up taking forty-five minutes longer than she had told them and when she got to the car, she was very embarrassed and they were very angry.

When thinking about this earlier situation where she was not the victim, but the perpetrator, she saw that she had many seemingly valid reasons (to her) why her actions should be excused. She had to check all the doors (no one else would have), made sure no one forgot their lunch, food, wallets, keys, homework, etc. (it was her job). She had to make sure the windows were shut and locked, all water faucets were completely turned off and that the dog had food and water for the day. With all that was going on for her, she felt that a mistake here and there should be forgiven. She then personally and deeply realized that people make mistakes. She also has made and makes mistakes. No one wants to make others wait and then make them angry. No one chooses to forget and overlook things. Rather, it is uncontrollable. Things happen, things get overlooked, and mistakes occur.

While we do not know why this person did what he did — whether on purpose or by accident — we do know that mistakes and situations like this happen. Since people are not all-perfect and all-knowing, mistakes will continue to happen. We do not need to forgive, but rather, we understand this Truth. She felt compassion and understanding for this person who made her wait. She understood the difficulties of being a fallible human in this flawed world. She understood that she herself would never want to intentionally hurt other people or herself. She would never want to setup a situation where someone would yell and reprimand her for something she did. She thought about how much getting yelled at for a mistake ruined her day and sometimes week.

She suddenly felt embarrassed for all the times she made others wait. She clearly understood and accepted the anger they felt towards her when she made them wait. She resolved to try her best to limit the time she would make people wait in the future. She would plan better and take the necessary steps to prevent future occurrences to the best of her ability. Yet, if it happened again, she would not beat herself up, but rather resolve to try again.

So when waiting, instead of steaming and thinking of how she would have told him off, she spent her time wisely and tried to think about all the other times she made people wait and how they turned out. She felt sorry for the people she hurt and felt sorry for herself, finally seeing that she was the cause of her hurt.

So when the man came and apologized for blocking her in, she merely smiled and said, it's ok, it happens. She felt compassion and loving-kindness for this being. She understood the plight of the human being. She didn't need to forgive him, she understood him — because she knew that she was no different from him.

If she were to punish him for his mistakes, then she would also have to punish herself for her mistakes, which she is generally unwilling to do. So, if I get a pass, then so do you.

This practice of Opanayiko is the practice of understanding others through understanding yourself. When you see you are no different than others, then you feel compassion for them, because you already feel compassion for yourself.

In another case, a young woman could never fully appreciate her mother or what her mother did for her. No matter how much she meditated and chanted, she could not get over the things she felt her mother did to her, the mean things her mother said to her, nor the bad decisions her mother made.

Then one day, the young woman gave birth to a baby girl. Every night she would cry and thank her mother softly while caring for her daughter. She never realized all the things her mother did for her or all the things her mother sacrificed for her to raise her. She finally knew, because she was going through essentially the same things her mother had. She now had perspective. She now had understanding. She now had appreciation and love for her mother.

This is an example of life forcing us to Opanayiko. However, if we wait for life to hand deliver parallels so that we can learn, it might be too late.

This is why the Buddha taught us to practice cultivating our wisdom (pañña). Wisdom can lead to compassion and understanding.

By merely trying to chant or force compassion, we are trying to generate a result without first creating the proper cause. We want a sexy body without eating properly and exercising. We want to be rich without working or sacrificing. We want love without having to do anything. This is not how things work. This world works based on cause and effect. Make the cause, receive the effect.

Therefore, by practicing compassion, loving-kindness and good-will through meditating, chanting or breathing, we are trying to force our souls to feel compassion. Instead, we should practice Opanayiko to give our souls and minds a reason to understand why we should be compassionate and have good will towards others.

I'M NOT GOOD AT READING TEXTBOOKS AND SCRIPTURES. DO I NEED TO DO A LOT OF STUDYING TO PRACTICE BUDDHISM?

YOU DO NOT HAVE to be a scholar to practice Buddhism. In fact, there were no schools or studying required during the Buddha's time. People would listen to teachings and take a snippet and go off privately and contemplate the Dhamma. They would compare it to their personal experiences, compare it to nature and the environment surrounding them, and would use their own logic and reasoning to discern. Then once they fully digested that snippet of Dhamma, they would come back for more. Often they would revisit the old snippet of Dhamma to see if there was anything more they can extract from it.

In fact, most of the teachings are just expositions of the four major teachings of the Buddha:

1. Middle Path (moderation, two sides)
2. Four Noble Truths (Suffering and how to end it)
3. Noble Eightfold Path (Method by which to end suffering)
4. Three Universal Characteristics (Suffering, Impermanence, No Self)

Armed with these four concepts, you have more than you need to practice Buddhism.

In fact, many people who study too much get confused and lost in the books, so much so that they forget to apply the teachings to themselves practically. In addition, too much book knowledge (textbook smarts) can lead to inflated egos and a sense of superiority (which is harmful to a Buddhist's practice).

Many people in the Buddha's day could not read, and were poor and uneducated. Yet they were able to grasp the Buddha's teachings. All they had to do was follow along in their minds and compare what the Buddha taught to what they have already experienced.

There was a daughter of a thread spinner who was carrying thread to her mother on the other side of town. As she crossed the town, she saw the Buddha sitting on a high seat preparing to give a sermon. He taught her that life is like a spool of thread. Whether small, medium, or thick, eventually it will all run out. The young girl, having a small lifetime of experience with thread, compared this statement to Truth. She found it to be completely true. Yet, in her whole life, she had never compared it to her own life, nor to the life of people around her. She immediately saw that some people die young (children), some people die in middle age (parents), and some people die in old age (grandparents). However, no matter when they die, everyone will die. Therefore, life is short and cannot be relied on. Therefore, her own clinging to life is impermanent and causing suffering. Once she saw this, she immediately freed her mind from the clinging to future rebirths and the desire within. She achieved the fruit of Stream-Entry.

Practicing Buddhism is as simple as investigating your daily thoughts and assumptions. Whichever thoughts lead to suffering and problems are thoughts that are based on a wrong view. Then, we intellectually contemplate what is wrong with our belief. Then we find what is right and replace our wrong view with that.

For example, let us assume that we are mad at our roommate for not doing things the way we like it done. We think our way is the best way. The way that they do it is improper and insufficient. This has led to numerous stare-downs, stressful encounters, passive aggressive scenarios, and arguments. We have tried numerous ways to try to coerce, to convince, to force, and to trick our roommate into doing it our way. We do not realize that our clinging to "our way is best" is the actual cause of our suffering. We want it a certain way, but does everyone? Obviously not.

There are many places and people on Earth with varying degrees of cleanliness and acceptability of dirtiness. There is no one way which is best. Each person does what that person is accustomed to and that fits their desires. In fact, there is no real difference between what we want and what they want.

We want them to be MORE clean. They want us to be MORE laid back. Who is right? If we use our standards, then we are right. If we use their standards, then we are wrong. There is no forcing us to live in a less clean situation (we find that unacceptable), just like they find it unacceptable that we are forcing our beliefs and standards onto them.

The wrong views that we hold are that our way is better, they should know and change, and that we can change them. Once we realize that these views are wrong, we can see that:

Our way is better in some situations, for some people. However, it is not always better.

They do not HAVE TO change. Their changing will both lead to our happiness and more suffering. What happens if they become a clean freak (more than you)? And now they are forcing you to clean at their new level? Who would suffer then?

We cannot change anyone. We can merely be a factor in their change. And if they do not want to change, we have no power to affect that change. The only change we can affect is our own.

Therefore, once we realize this, we can simply just clean to the level we want, for ourselves, without thinking of getting others to change or to adjust. We like it a certain way, and we do it that way, for ourselves. But if the situation changes and what we do creates a new suffering, we are willing to adjust.

I HEAR A LOT OF BUDDHISTS TALK ABOUT ABHIDHAMMA. WHAT IS IT? DO I NEED TO KNOW ABOUT IT?

....

A FEW YEARS AFTER THE BUDDHA began teaching the Dhamma, he spent an entire rains retreat (about three months) in the Tavatimsa heaven. He went there for the purpose of teaching the Dhamma to his mother, who passed away shortly after giving birth to him. The teachings were designed for the celestial beings, the devas, and other beings in the heavens. Each day, the Buddha would briefly return to the human realm to collect alms and he would, upon request from Sariputta, transmit that day's portion of what he just preached. The collection of teachings that were given to the formless beings were collected and compiled and came to be known as the Abhidhamma.

Acariya Thoon told us not to bother with Abhidhamma. If the Buddha thought the Abhidhamma was accessible for humans (those with physical form) he would have taught it directly to his human students. The Buddha never did this, not even in one instance. The reason for this, Acariya Thoon explained, was that as humans, we must first shed our attachment to our physical form before shedding our attachment to our non-physical form. The devas and spiritual beings did not have a physical form. Therefore, the Buddha taught them teachings that are for those who do not have physical form. He told us that contemplating the physical form is hard enough to do. Any attempt to contemplate the non-physical form without first contemplating the physical form is egotistical and foolish.

In my opinion, this is akin to men studying women's anatomy and trying to apply it to themselves. Men and women are different; therefore, the medicine and constructs that are designed for a women's body, will not fully work properly when applied to a man's body. A man must study the anatomy of a man in order to properly apply that knowledge to himself. The same goes for women.

I HAVE A PROBLEM WITH BELIEVING IN REBIRTH, SINCE THERE IS NO PHYSICAL OR SCIENTIFIC EVIDENCE OF AN AFTERLIFE.

MANY PEOPLE HAVE A PROBLEM with believing in rebirth and past and future lives. Even without believing in rebirth, one can still practice Buddhism and achieve good results. Buddhism teaches doing good and improving yourself now, in addition to for future lives. But even if you don't believe in rebirth, the techniques that Buddhism teaches for improving oneself can be very helpful for your present life.

Not being fully able to accept the concept of rebirth is a common problem for many people. Usually with Buddhism, faith is not a guiding component. In general, the Buddha teaches that if we follow his teachings correctly, we will be able to fully understand the Truth by ourselves. Therefore, faith is not the determining factor of spiritual progress in Buddhism. However, it is difficult to take things that we cannot see, like heaven and hell, afterlives, rebirth, or karma, at face value.

However, we do not have to take them at face value. There are many things that we cannot see that exist. For example, gravity is something we cannot see, yet we have no trouble accepting that it exists. Air is something we cannot see, yet we know that it exists. Then again, unicorns are something we cannot see since they do not exist. So what is the difference?

How do we know that gravity exists? Well, there has to be some reason that heavy things fall to the ground. There has to be some force explaining why when you let go of something heavy, it travels towards the ground instead of up into the air. Everywhere we look, we can see the effects of gravity. Therefore, there is enough supporting evidence for us to know that gravity exists.

How do we know that tomorrow will actually come? We have no physical proof that tomorrow will exist, because it is in the future, it hasn't happened yet. Therefore, there is no way to prove that tomorrow will exist. On the other hand, yesterday existed. We know this as a fact. We know that the day before yesterday existed and the day before that. We know that each day before that existed due to our own knowledge of our existence. We even know of our existence as a child and baby since we are told of it, pictures of us exist, and others were affected by our existence. We know that the time before our birth existed because there were stories written, memories shared, and also due to logical rationale that the past existed. Because every day in our past is followed by its respective "tomorrow," we safely assume that our own "tomorrow" will come to pass. We have no actual proof, yet there is sufficient evidence to allow us to know that time continues and does not randomly stop and start. There has been no proof of the opposite.

How do we know that we will die one day? It has not happened yet. Yet, every living being that has ever lived has eventually died. Those that are alive are all moving towards the end of their lives. There has never been a single person who was born who did not eventually die. Therefore, it is safe to assume and believe that we too will eventually die.

The same thinking applies to rebirth. Everything in the world constantly changes form. Nothing stays in one form forever. After it leaves one form, it becomes another. For example, a seed floats in the wind. Eventually it lands on some dirt. The seed begins to grow into a small plant. The seed can no longer be found. The small plant grows into a large tree. The small plant can no longer be found. Eventually the large tree grows old, dies, and falls back to the ground. Now the large living tree can no longer be found. The tree is now a dry log. Eventually the log becomes soil and fertilizer and returns to the ground. The drying log can no longer be found. At every death, a new role takes its place. At the end of that role, another role replaces it. Nothing ever stops changing forms and changing roles. As we search the entire universe and everything we know to be in it, we see that everything moves towards another form. One form begets another. One role changes into another. Since everything in the world works this way, it logically follows that our souls will follow the same pattern.

Rebirth works the same way. As we finish one life, we move on to another. At the end of that one, we move to another life. Each life is separate, yet related in that the soul occupying that life is influenced by the experiences and knowledge acquired by the soul in the past lives.

I OFTEN HEAR BUDDHISTS TALK ABOUT LETTING THINGS GO. HOW DOES ONE JUST SIMPLY LET IT GO? IT SOUNDS SO SIMPLE BUT IS SO HARD TO DO

THIS IS ANOTHER CASE OF PEOPLE trying to practice a result. In other words, they are trying to force a result to happen. This is not how it works. In order to let something go, the Buddha said that we must practice according to the Noble Eightfold Path and the Four Noble Truths.

The Four Noble Truths tell us that suffering occurs because of a cause. That cause can be identified and fixed. Once fixed, the resulting suffering will cease as well. The only method the Buddha taught to fix the cause is the Noble

Eightfold Path, and then primarily the first step, Right View. Our suffering is due to our wrong views. Therefore, we must change them to Right Views. Once we know Right View, our suffering will cease. Right View is classified by three simple universal Truths:

1. All things are impermanent. (Annicam)
2. Trying to make impermanent things permanent will lead to suffering. (Suffering)
3. Since all things are impermanent, we cannot extract a permanent sense of self from that which is impermanent. (Anatta)

To simplify, in order to truly let go of something, we must use the tools we have already talked about here:

1. Experience the Suffering that comes from our wrong view. (Dukkha)
2. Realize the wrong view comes from us and not from others. (Opanayiko)

3. Identify why our view is considered wrong by comparing it to the Law of Impermanence. (Micchaditthi)
4. Discern what the Right View is and replace our Wrong View. (Sammaditthi)

Acariya Thoon once relayed a parable for us. Imagine reaching into a large water jug of submerged apples. Each time you pull out an apple, you will be happy and confident that each attempt will result in the same manner — an apple. Now imagine if on your next attempt you pulled out a snake instead of an apple. What would you do? Do you have to be trained to "let it go?" No, you will fling that snake away as far away as you can. Why? Because we know that snakes contain peril and dange. It is too risky and too dangerous to hold on for too long.

Letting things go is much the same way. Instead of practicing letting go, we must instead practice wisdom in order to understand the danger and perils associated with things in this world. Once we know the dangers that are connected to attachment, we will be unable and unwilling to be heedless and careless when dealing with that attachment. We will not need to be taught how to let the attachment go; we will instinctively know it ourselves.

A practitioner offers the following story about letting go:

I really like drinking coffee. It is delicious and makes me feel alert. However, when I started having stomach problems, I noticed that coffee made it much worse. After a single cup I would be in pain. Even though I still enjoyed the taste and alertness, it wasn't worth the pain. I didn't meditate on giving it up, I casually let it go because I thought it was bad. I saw the cost, in my own life, and I gave it up.

Chapter Six

BUDDHISM IN ACTION

FATHER ISSUES

....

Ever since I was a little child, I harbored a strong resentment for my father and his lack of proficiency in English. I based my disappointment on the fact that he had been here for over 30 years and still did not bother to learn the language or accent. He still spoke broken English like someone who had just come over, not someone who had been here for over 30 years. My mom told me the many reasons why he did this, but I never allowed myself to forgive or forget the embarrassment I felt whenever I had my friends over or when I had to bring him to a school or social function. I held this anger deep inside for many years, but became proficient at keeping it restrained and preventing it from surfacing. It all stemmed from the belief that my father REFUSED to learn English even though there was no good reason not to.

To understand this story better, it might help you to know a little bit about me. I was born and raised as a Thai-American in San Francisco. For many years, I took summer classes from the Thai temple, learning how to read and write in the Thai language. However, it has been over 20 years since then. I speak Thai 90% fluently, yet have never took the time to become proficient in reading and writing Thai. With my current language skill level, I can give fluent sermons in Thai and English, I can communicate with any Thai person, and can travel alone in Thailand without any problems.

One day a few years ago, there was a situation at my temple. We have a donation board near the entrance of the temple with a list of donors who pledge monthly support for the temple. A man asked if his name could be added to the board, and I said yes. He then asked if someone else could write his name on the board for him (in Thai). As I looked around, there were no lay people available to help me. He then said he wanted me to write his name on the board for him. At this point, I was embarrassed to tell him that I could not write Thai. I thought of the resentment I harbored for my dad. I always thought that he REFUSED to learn English. I realized that this guy or anyone else could easily accuse me of the same thing. They could say that I REFUSED to learn how to read and write Thai. My mind immediately came up with numerous excuses and reasons why I had not learned how to read and write Thai over the years. All of my reasons and excuses seemed extremely valid and justified.

I was full of feelings. I felt embarrassed and frustrated. I was feeling nervous and scared. I had all these feelings from someone asking me to do something I couldn't do well. I realized this feeling was not something I enjoyed, nor wanted to experience. If my reasons and excuses were valid to me, his reasons and excuses were valid to him. If I had the right to choose not to master Thai, then he also had the right to choose not to master English — regardless of the situation or reasons. I never realized how it felt to be on the receiving end of the pressure. But now that I knew, I was embarrassed that I was imposing this onto another human being, especially one that I claimed to love.

At that moment, my heart melted, and all the resentment I harbored melted away like an iceberg in the face of global warming. All anger was replaced with embarrassment and resolve. I realized my wrong views not only caused me anger and suffering, but also caused others suffering, which in turn will lead to more suffering for me.

So to clarify:

What was being held: Anger for father's English

Suffering experienced: Anger and embarrassment whenever the situations arose or when I thought about it.

Source of the problem (cause): I believed he REFUSED to learn English with no valid reason not to. (My judgment is the best and most valid)

Wrong View: there is no exuces for not knowing how to do something.

Internalize: There are things that I am not adept at. I have reasons why this is so. These reasons are valid to me.

New Understanding: Everyone has their own reasons and opinions as to why they do or do not do something. My views and opinions are not always best for everyone. Sometimes they are good for others, sometimes they are not.

Right View: Imposing my views as the law of the land violates the Law of Impermanence. My beliefs are not the only ones that are right and applicable in all situations. In addition, imposing my beliefs on others can lead to suffering for them, and for myself.

MCDONALD'S

....

A **FAMILY OF THREE WAS SEARCHING** for a place to eat during Chinese New Years in Thailand. As they were searching, they found most of the restaurants to be closed, as was customary for this holiday. The only open restaurant they found was McDonald's.

A little background information first: The wife and husband had spent a lot of time in the United States during the time they were earning their bachelor degrees. After about ten years, they moved back to Thailand and had a daughter. The husband was Thai-Chinese. His family observed

Chinese traditions, which included not eating beef. The wife was well aware of this fact.

As they pulled into the McDonald's, the husband and daughter planned to stay in the car while the wife went to get the food.

The wife asked the husband, "What do you want to eat?"

The husband looked out the window at the menu posted outside McDonald's and said, "I'll have the Big Mac."

The wife looked surprised and turned and asked, "Honey, you want a Big Mac?"

The husband checked the menu again and said, "Yes, I'll have the Big Mac."

The wife looked even more incredulous and said, "Honey, are you really, really sure you want to eat a Big Mac?"

The husband said with increasing frustration, "Yes, I said Big Mac."

The wife looked extremely confused and said, "Honey, are you absolutely sure you want to order a Big Mac?"

The husband responded with anger, "Yes, I said Big Mac, stop asking me and go get it!"

The wife angrily left the car and went to place that order. When she returned, she gave her daughter her order and gave her husband the Big Mac. As he unwrapped it and prepared to take a bite, he looked at it, examined it, and turned to his wife and said, "How long have you known me? When have you ever known me to eat beef? Why would you buy me beef?"

The wife turned to her husband, seething with anger. She felt ready to explode. But before she said or did anything, she remembered a teaching a Mae Chee (a nun) once gave her.

The Mae Chee had said, "Whenever you are angry, you are the one who is wrong. You must find the wrong in yourself and once you do, the anger will subside."

The woman reminded herself of this teaching and held her tongue. But she felt like her insides were about to burst! She wanted to say and do so many things, but knew better. So she kept it inside. When they got home, she picked up the phone and called the Mae Chee (in America) and relayed the entire story. As the Mae Chee listened, she responded with a simple question, "I don't understand, what is a Big Mac? Is it beef? Can it be chicken or pork or fish?"

The wife was stupefied. "Mae Chee, how could you not know? You've lived in the United States for over 45 years! Your children eat McDonald's all the time!"

The Mae Chee answered, "But I don't eat McDonald's; I never have."

At this point, the woman completely understood her misperception. She had assumed that since she knew the Big Mac was made out of beef that everyone else MUST also know that the Big Mac must be made out of beef. That is why she kept repeatedly asking her husband if he wanted to eat a Big Mac instead of asking him if he wanted to eat beef. To her, a Big Mac was obviously beef. Since she knew this, why wouldn't he? She immediately knew that this entire situation arose because of a wrong viewpoint, a wrong perception that she held. Once she realized this, she realized that she had no one else to blame for this situation other than herself.

If she had held the right viewpoint, her actions would have been different. She still might have asked him the first time if he wanted a Big Mac, but after a second time, she would probably rephrase the question:

"Did you know a Big Mac is made out of beef?"

Or

"Did you want to order beef?"

Any of these questions would have resulted in a clearer answer and therefore would have most likely resulted in a different and less stressful situation.

So why didn't the wife ask any of these questions? Owing to her (wrong) viewpoint, knowing that a Big Mac was made of beef was implied. It wasn't necessary to explain. Everyone in the whole world (it sounds silly when we say it like this — hindsight is 20/20) knows that Big Macs are made out of beef. To have to say beef is redundant. Once the wrong viewpoint takes a hold of our minds, we cannot help but make assumptions and say things presumptuously.

So in the end, the Mae Chee was right. The one who is angry is the one who is wrong. The one who gets angry is holding a wrong viewpoint. Once we find the wrong viewpoint, we will become aware of our fault and take the steps to fix it. The anger will subside, since our anger originally comes from blaming the responsible party. However, now we know that the responsible party is we ourselves. We are less likely to get angry at ourselves. Now the next step is to fix the wrong viewpoint and prevent future occurrences. We will use the suffering of this situation to highlight the dangers, perils and suffering resulting from this wrong viewpoint so that we remember this lesson.

So to clarify:

What was being held: Anger for husband who was being stubborn.

Suffering experienced: Anger, frustration, stress, and shock.

Source of the problem (cause): We believe that because I know something to be true or correct, that other people will also know it to be true or correct.

Wrong View: If I know, then so do others. It seems certain.

Contemplation: Is it necessary that if I know something to be true and correct that others will always know it too? In what situations will I know something that others do not? In what situations will others know something that I do not? In what situations will I know something that others also know? In what situations will others know something that I also know? In what situations is what I know not correct?

New Understanding: Just because I know something to be true and correct does not always mean that others are privy to the same knowledge. Even if they were next to me when I learned it, or even if they had ample opportunity to learn it, this is not enough for me to conclude that they will have the same knowledge and experience that I do.

Right View: If I know, others might know or they might not know. It is not certain.

POST-IT NOTE

I HAD ONLY BEEN GONE from my desk for about 3 minutes. When I returned to my desk, I saw a post it note on my desk. When I looked down at the note, it said, Person A called. Please call her back. Once I read the note, I felt anger flushing over me.

Without having to look at the contents of the note, I knew immediately who had left it. It was my coworker whose desk was right next to mine. I felt upset and annoyed. I had learned from my Dhamma teachers that once we are angry, our practice has begun.

The first step was to identify if I was mad at the person or the action. So I used the swapping heads technique I learned at the last retreat.

First I imagined this person doing the action. Was I still mad? Yes.

Then I imagined someone else doing the action. Was I still mad? Yes.

Even though I am generally annoyed with this coworker's personality, I realize that in this particular case, it was the action that made me angry.

Now that I know it is the action, I must now figure out its cause. To do this, I use questions.

I asked myself, why was I angry? The answer I received was that I don't know, I just am. Not too clear and not too much to work with.

My teachers told me that I must change the question in this case.

When I tried again, I asked myself what could have happened that would have resulted in my not being angry?

Then, the answer was clear.

I wanted to talk to the person who called, when they called. I did not want to call back. I wanted the coworker to have told the person to hold on, since I was back in 3 minutes. The wait wouldn't have been longer than a few moments.

At this point, I found my cause (perception). I wanted things to be a certain way. And most importantly, I wanted my coworker to do it the way I wanted.

At this point I asked myself, "is my perception correct?"

I then used impermanence to contemplate the validity of my perception.

I was mad because the person who called was someone I wanted to talk to.

If a person that I normally like calls, will I want to pick up the phone?

Well, in general I would want to talk to people I care about. For example, I would want to talk to my mother, sister, best friends, and boyfriend. However, there are also times when they call that I DO NOT want to answer the phone. Sometimes I am not ready to talk to them for various reasons. Other times, I just don't feel like talking to them.

So even with someone I normally care for, it is not certain I will always want to talk to them. It really depends on many factors, especially how I feel at the present moment.

If a person I normally don't want to talk to calls, will I want to pick up the phone?

Typically, if people I don't like (ex-boyfriends, enemies, solicitors, debt collectors) call, I would not want to speak to them. However, there are those few moments when I would. For example, the ex-boyfriends who were calling to return something I really wanted back, enemies calling to apologize, or a solicitor calling to offer me something I actually want. Even though it is not often, there are some cases that I would want to talk to these "no-talk" people.

So even with people I don't like, it is not certain I will never want to talk to them. It also depends on my many factors, especially how I am feeling at the current moment.

In the case where I want to talk to them and instead I see a Post-it note, I would be mad.

In the case where I do not want to talk to them and instead I see a Post-it note, I would be thankful.

I realized that even I could not determine ahead of time whether I would or would not want to talk to a variety of people. How could it be possible for someone else (especially my coworker) to know exactly how I am feeling at the moment and then act completely according to that feeling that I have? The simple answer is, it is crazy to expect that.

My desire to have other people do what I want, when I want it, and how I want is, is absurd. If even I can't always know my moods, how could I expect others to know them? They can't!

I realized my anger from not getting what I want is foolish since my desire to have others know my mind is completely foolish. At this realization, my anger subsided and embarrassment at my foolishness replaced it. I know the next time I get angry at situations like this, I will know to look inwards and see what desires I am holding and to check their sensibility.

ABOUT THE AUTHOR

A**NANDAPANYO** B**HIKKHU** (A**RNOLD** T**HIAN-**N**GERN**) is a first-generation Thai-American, born and raised in San Francisco. He was raised Buddhist, and is fluent in both Thai and English.

Throughout his adolescence, Arnold studied many religions, and experimented in various Buddhist traditions. However, none could quench his thirst for true understanding. After meeting Acariya Thoon Khippapanyo, a modern day Enlightened Thai monk, this quest for truth finally began to gain traction. He spent ten years studying under Acariya Thoon and his disciples, gaining insight into the techniques in wisdom-based practice, and decided to ordain in 2009. He was given the monk name of Anandapanyo, meaning "immense wisdom."

As San Fran Dhammaram Temple's resident English-speaking monk, Anandapanyo Bhikkhu has dedicated his time to sharing Acariya Thoon's teachings with the greater public. Anandapanyo Bhikkhu frequently travels overseas to give sermons and put on Dhamma retreats.

Upon noticing the common questions asked by new practitioners, Anandapanyo Bhikkhu decided to compile those questions into an easy to understand book. This introduction to Buddhism series is a great way to ease into the culture and teachings of wisdom-based Buddhism.

ACKNOWLEDGMENTS

I WOULD LIKE TO EXPRESS MY SINCERE GRATITUDE to all my teachers, for without them, my Dhamma practice would be impossible.

I am most grateful to the Lord Buddha, who provided the Noble Eightfold Path for us to follow. Without him the path to eliminate our suffering would be unknown.

I am eternally grateful to my teacher, Venerable Acariya Thoon Khippapanyo, who led me down that path and saved me from wasting valuable years of my life practicing incorrectly.

I am forever indebted to Mae Yo for breathing life into my body and my soul. My mother is my inspiration, my example, my guide, my teacher, and my friend. She has given me everything I will ever need in my practice; all that remains is for me to do it.

I would like to thank my sister and Dhamma teacher Neecha Thian-Ngern. Thank you for being patient and straightforward with me during my practice. In addition, thank you for helping to check content and edit language in each of my books.

I would like to thank the Abbott of San Fran Dhammaram Temple, Phra Nut Nuttapanyo. Your technical expertise and attentiveness really made this book happen.

I would like to thank all my Dhamma friends. I have learned so much from your Dhamma journey. I am grateful to Alana Denison, Jason Konik, and John Sum for their valuable edits, comments, and stories in this book. It was very refreshing to have other people look at my work and provide constructive feedback; it allowed me to see all the mistakes I made. Without seeing my mistakes, I would never be able to improve.

Lastly, I'd like to thank the ever-talented Tanawat Pisanuwongse for the cover design and invaluable artistic input.